BLUEGRASS MASTERS

Kenny Baker
fiddle

by David Brody

Oak Publications
New York • London • Tokyo • Sydney • Cologne

For my parents.

Acknowledgements

I am greatly indebted to Matt Glaser for his many thoughtful suggestions, Jules Brody for his editorial help, and to Melodie Janis who was so good as to type, retype, and re-retype this manuscript, saving me much time and aggravation.

I would also like to thank Ronnie Bauch, Bob Carlin, Rollo Mortez, Hank Sapoznik, Dave Freeman, Peter Kuykendall, and the patient folks at Oak: Halley, Peter, and Jason.

It only remains for me to thank Kenny, who supplied much of the material for this book.

Photo Credits

John Lee   front cover
Herb Wise   back cover
Country Music Foundation   14
Carl Fleischhauer   13
David Gahr   4, 40
Eric Levenson   5, 20
Phil Straw   37, 67
Photos on pages 6 and 26 are courtesy of Kenny Baker.

Book and cover design by Barbara Hoffman
Edited by Halley Gatenby and Jason Shulman
Music edited by Peter Pickow

e d c b a

© Oak Publications, 1979
A Division of Embassy Music Corporation, New York
All Rights Reserved

International Standard Book Number: 0-8256-0224-6
Library of Congress Catalog Card Number: 78-74572

Distributed throughout the world by Music Sales Corporation:

33 West 60th Street, New York 10023
78 Newman Street, London W1P 3LA
4-26-22 Jingumae, Shibuya-ku, Tokyo 150
27 Clarendon Street, Artarmon, Sydney NSW
Kölner Strasse 199, 5000 Cologne 90

Contents

Foreword 4
Introduction 5
Biography 6
Stylistic Analysis 7
   The Bow 7
   Phrasing 8
   The Left Hand 9
   Playing Variations 10
Music Notation 11
   Slides and Ornaments 11
   Reading the Transcriptions 12
   How to Use the Transcriptions 13
The Tunes 14
   Big Sandy River 14
   Bluegrass in the Backwoods 17
   Charmaine 20
   Cross-Eyed Fiddler 24
   Dead March 26
   Denver Belle 28
   Doc Harris the Fisherman 30
   Done Gone 33
   Dry and Dusty 36
   Ducks on the Millpond 37
   Festival Waltz 40
   First Day in Town 43
   Flopareno 45
   Grey Eagle 50
   Indian Killed a Woodcock 53
   Johnny the Blacksmith 55
   Lee Wedding Tune 57
   Missouri Road 59
   Mule Skinner Blues 61
   Sail Away Ladies 65
   Salty 67
   Spider Bit the Baby 70
Discography 72

Foreword

I've never been too good at explaining to people how I do what I do. I could probably take my fiddle out and show them, but to explain in words, no. Then too, a lot of fiddlers with more education in music than I ever had ask me where they can find sheet music on what I've recorded, but up to now I could never help them.

Suddenly here comes David Brody with the interest and the knowledge and the patience to put all this down on paper, and there's actually a company ready to publish something like this all about my music. From now on when people ask me those kinds of questions I'll be able to refer them to this book. I know having it available for that will be a real benefit to me. I trust it will also be a real benefit to those educated musicians who find they can grasp music better when it's written down.

Kenny Baker

Kenny with Bill Monroe, Newport Folk Festival, 1969.

Introduction

The majority of the tunes in this book are taken from Kenny's solo albums on the County label. I have chosen fourteen original and five traditional tunes from these recordings. The rest are transcriptions of sessions that Kenny taped with the Bluegrass Boys.

The degree of prominence that Kenny has achieved in country music is easily ascertainable at any large fiddle contest or bluegrass festival, where you can be sure to hear someone playing his tunes. You might even see a crowd clustered around two fiddlers trading licks on "High Country," a double-fiddle piece which Kenny recorded on his first County album with Joe Greene. Such tunes as "Big Sandy River" and "Festival Waltz" form an integral part of the bluegrass fiddler's repertoire and have come to be regarded as classics. Other tunes which Kenny has written more recently, like "Bluegrass in the Backwoods," are sure to become classics in time. Since his early days with Bill Monroe he has come to be regarded as one of the leading exponents of bluegrass fiddle playing. He has composed and recorded more bluegrass instrumentals than perhaps any other fiddler, and for these reasons has a profound effect on serious students of bluegrass music.

Biography

On June 26th, 1926, Kenneth Clayton Baker was born to Myrtle and T.E. (Thaddeus Earl) Baker, in the coal mining town of Jenkins, Kentucky. As far back as he can remember Kenny heard the sound of traditional fiddling. "My daddy played the fiddle something along the line of Arthur Smith... and my grandmother and grandfather [on his father's side] played something like... you know the way Tommy Jarrell plays? ... well, something like that."

Kenny started learning to play the fiddle at an early age but, as he relates, was scantily encouraged by his father. "He said I'd never learn to play the thing." Kenny took up the guitar instead.

When he was seventeen, Kenny joined the navy and played guitar in a small dance band while stationed in Okinawa. He remained in the service until 1946, and in March of that year returned to Jenkins where he went to work in the mines. It was at that time that Kenny started playing the fiddle seriously.

By 1949 Kenny had joined a local group. They didn't have a name, but they didn't seem to need one. "We were the only band around, everyone knew who'd be playing." In 1953 he left the mines, and his local band, to work for Don Gibson, a country singer. This was Kenny's first full-time job playing fiddle. He worked with Don until 1957, with one short interruption in 1954 to play with the Bailey Brothers.

In 1957 Bill Monroe, who had been trying to get Kenny to come and play with the Bluegrass Boys for a few years, finally succeeded. Kenny has played with Bill on and off for a period of over twenty years, going back to work in the mines at various times in his life in order to be at home more often with his family.

Since 1967, when he recorded his first album for County Records, Kenny has had a career as a solo artist paralleling his work with Bill. It is with these recordings (eight albums, and a ninth forthcoming) that Kenny has firmly established himself as one of the great bluegrass fiddlers of our time.

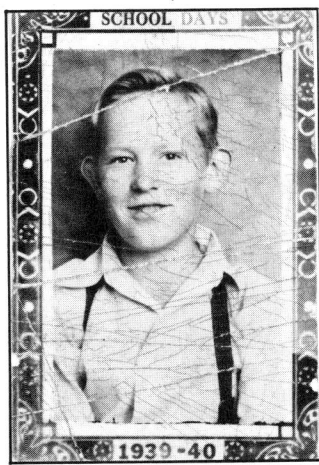

Kenny (center) with his brothers Earl (left) and Carl.

Stylistic Analysis

The Bow

If a single adjective had to be chosen to describe Kenny's bowing style, it would have to be "smooth." Kenny first encountered this type of bowing, which he calls his "long bow" style, in his father's playing.

In most old-time music the basic bow-stroke is the "shuffle," consisting of one long bow, followed by two short ones. A double stop is often played on the first of the two shorts, to effect an accent.

The shuffle in its most basic form sounds like this when applied to a melody, the first few bars of "Sally Goodin":

In this pattern, beats 1 and 3 are naturally accented; 3 a bit more than 1. This type of bowing is the antithesis of a smooth, flowing style because the accents reinforce the rhythmic divisions and subdivisions that are naturally heard in a group of running eighth or sixteenth notes in duple or quadruple meter (indicated by brackets below).

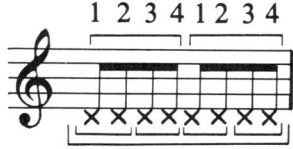

To create a smooth bowing pattern, connect the otherwise separate beats, bridging with the bow those natural divisions. If Kenny were to play the above melody from "Sally Goodin," it would be well in keeping with his style to bow it like this:

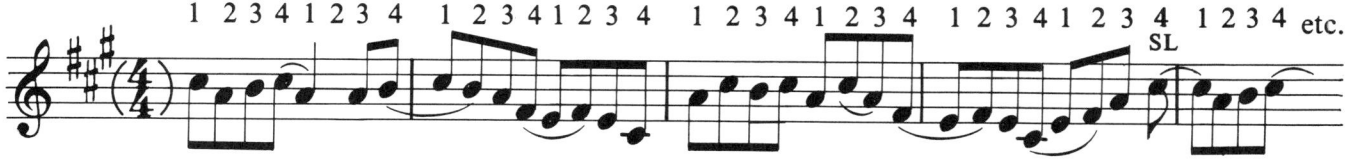

7

Inside the measure itself, beats 2 and 3, and 4 and 1, are often connected. Whole measures are bridged by playing 4 of the first measure with the same bow-stroke as 1 and 2 of the second measure. Likewise, entire musical phrases are often linked by anticipating the first note of the second phrase in the last note of the first phrase, as seen above in measures four to five. (See "Big Sandy River," page 15, measures sixteen and seventeen.)

Shortly before the turn of the century the guitar was introduced into Southern music. Before then, the fiddle was used primarily as a dance instrument, supplying a steady and insistent rhythm. This limited its movement into more melodic and harmonic areas, and restricted its use of varied accent patterns. The development of the New England fiddler was different because he had that pulse, necessary for dancing, supplied by piano. It was perhaps for this reason that Northern style dance fiddling developed in a more melodic and ornamental direction, the shuffle playing only a small role.

Once the guitar became easily obtainable in the South, new styles of fiddle playing began to be heard. These shied away from a rhythmic pattern which essentially accented beats 1 and 3, and tended instead towards a more flowing melody line. Arthur Smith and Posey Rorer (a fiddler who played with the infamous Charlie Poole) were early exponents of this style, while Gid Tanner represented an opposing attitude.

Kenny uses only one other bowing pattern with any great regularity—the saw stroke, which is a simple pattern of a single stroke for each note. It is difficult to achieve Kenny's smooth, flowing sound using this pattern. Some suggestions for achieving this smoothness are found in the introduction to "Big Sandy River."

Phrasing

The kind of rhythmic freedom that Kenny enjoys is closely related to the steadiness of his backup. Whether playing with the Bluegrass Boys, or on his own County albums, the rhythm sustained by the guitar, bass, mandolin, and banjo gives him a solid foundation upon which to build his breaks. In the introductions to the various tunes, I will point out many of the interesting ways in which Kenny organizes phrases. He often relies on the use of dotted and syncopated rhythms, and upon a shifting of the musical phrase so that it is no longer confined by the bar line. Such rhythmic devices are common in bluegrass—they make up an essential part of Bill Monroe's mandolin style, for example. They are also an important ingredient in jazz fiddling—Kenny is particularly interested in Stephane Grappelli's playing.

In "Festival Waltz," the first note, the upbeat, is an A, followed by a downbeat in the first measure, a C♯.

In measure five, ostensibly a repeat of the above phrase, the melodic content has been retained, but its relationship to the bar line has been altered.

In measures thirty-two through thirty-six of the same piece, there is another interesting juxtaposition of bar line to melody. The apparent divisions are made by the bar line, but the phrasing causes the aural—or musical—divisions to occur quite differently (as indicated by the brackets).

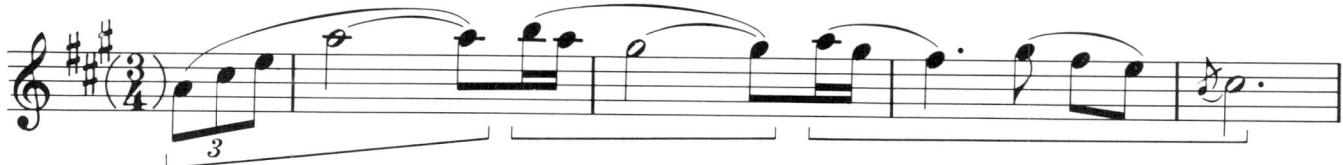

The Left Hand

Kenny uses a good deal of the fingerboard. He often plays in third and fourth positions, and less often in second position. The use of these positions came late into country music partially because the traditional dance tunes that require shifting are few. It wasn't until the twenties and thirties that changing positions became at all common practice. At that time it was used primarily to lengthen the scale on the E string so that it would be possible to play a high melody. An example of this is Arthur Smith's version of "There's More Pretty Girls Than One," recorded in the mid-thirties. (Reissued on RCA Vintage series *Smoky Mountain Ballads* LPV-507.)

Kenny often plays a high melody, or high melodic variation—listen to the first A part of "Spider Bit the Baby," and parts C, D, E, F, and G of "Grey Eagle." He also plays many double-stop inversions which are only possible in positions other than first. For instance, in measures sixty-three through sixty-seven of "Mule Skinner Blues," Kenny pulls off a difficult and highly syncopated variation, played in double stops in second position. In "Flopareno" he slides from one double stop to the next, playing different inversions of the same chord (c.f. measure nine). On the whole, Kenny uses double stops with a harmonic rather than a rhythmic intent, unlike many of the old-timers.

It is astounding that Kenny supports the greater part of the weight of his violin in the palm of his left hand, yet consistently shifts and intones accurately. The effect of such a posture on most fiddlers is that the hand's ability to change position is greatly hampered by the instrument's cumbersome weight. Many musicians would avoid this problem by securely holding the violin between the shoulder and the chin, and using a shoulder rest to better fit the violin to the slope of the shoulder. (The Resonans shoulder rest is very popular.)

Another stylistic feature of Kenny's playing is his use of chromaticism. In his own tunes, the melody itself often contains a short chromatic passage. (See measure fifteen of "Bluegrass in the Backwoods," and measure forty-five of "Salty.") In his adaptations of traditional and pop tunes he often adds such a passage as well. (See measure twenty-three of "Done Gone," and measure eleven of "Charmaine.")

Playing Variations

Many musicians learn a piece and continue to play it just as they learned it forever more. Kenny comments upon this attitude in an interview with David Freeman, "Mechanical fiddlers apply themselves to learn that number one way and they'll never change, not one phrase, not one note, nothing about it. Every time they play it—whether they feel up to playing it or whether they don't—it's exactly the same. They work out their patterns and they set their notes in there and that's exactly what they play ten years from today."

Kenny can be characterized as a musician who plays from the heart and who, at the same time, has an intuitive sense of order that transforms his feelings into an artful form. These are the feelings that dictate his approach to a tune, and this is perhaps why Kenny rarely plays a tune the same way twice, often playing many variations around the original melody. Unlike many musicians who, when playing an improvised line, float off into a somewhat chaotic string of unrelated tones which is invariably less forcefully stated than the melody itself, Kenny always plays a variation with such conviction that it sounds as if it had been a part of the piece since its conception. This forceful sound is due partially to his technical control of the instrument, but also to the highly structured form that his breaks follow.

Music Notation

Slides and Ornaments

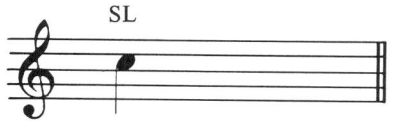
Slide up into the note indicated from a pitch slightly below.

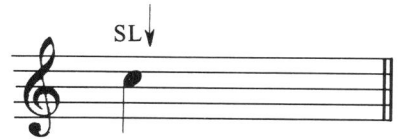
Slide down into the note indicated from a pitch slightly above.

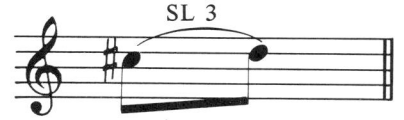
Slide with the indicated finger from the first pitch to the second.

Same as the above, but now in the opposite direction.

Basically equivalent to this symbol is used because the structure which it represents is ornamental. It also facilitates reading through the deletion of sixteenth notes.

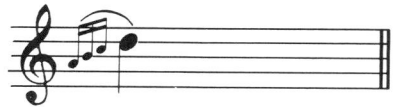
The three notes in small print are *grace notes* and are considered as a rhythmic part of the note which they precede.

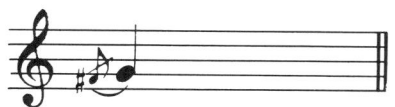
The single grace note is also considered as a rhythmic part of the note which it precedes. Listen to the recordings to get a firm idea of how both the single and triple grace note should sound.

Reading the Transcriptions

Due to space limitations I have not transcribed each piece in its entirety. Instead, I have devised a shorthand form which facilitates the presentation of the tune as a whole, and enables you to follow along in the transcription from beginning to end while listening to the recordings.
If you were to read through "Missouri Road" (page 59), for example, you would begin at the first A part. Moving directly along you would breeze through part B and soon arrive at A2. Because its content is quite similar to that of A, I have chosen not to include it in its full form, but rather to indicate its similarities and differences to A in a section of notes following the tune (see page 60). Upon consulting these notes, you fill find that A parts 2 and 4 ≈ A, but in A2 measures 1, 5, and 9 are played without double stops:

(I have chosen the symbol ≈ which means "approximately equal to" to show similarity between parts; no two parts ever being played identically.)

Because A2 is like A, back-track and follow along in that part. B2 is fully transcribed because it is unlike any section yet played. So read through it and, forging onwards, you arrive at A3. Here again you must refer to the notes; A3 is similar to A, so go back and re-read A. At B3 you must, according to the notes, read once again through B, B3 being ≈ B. Earlier in these proceedings you found out, while foraging in the notes for information pertaining to A2, that A4 was also similar to A, so for a third time you venture backwards to that first A and now, quite at home with these sixteen bars, you can follow along with ease. You eventually arrive at B4, and discover that B4 is like B except in one particular: the phrase in measures twenty-three and twenty-four is played differently from that in B, and so is transcribed and appears under the verbal explanation. You must then go back and read through B making the necessary substitution for measures twenty-three and twenty-four, and continuing forward ultimately reach the end tag plainly written out at the end of B4.

How to Use the Transcriptions

I can hardly stress enough the importance of listening to the recordings of the tunes contained in this volume, because there is a dimension to any performer's playing that is nontranscribable. The same transcription, however accurate, when played by two individuals, may very well sound like two different pieces. To pick up on this "extra something" which gives the piece its life and personality, listen, listen, listen!

In proceeding to learn one of Kenny's tunes, I suggest that you:

1. Listen to the piece until you are able to hum a decent outline of the tune. Pay attention to modulations, double stop sections, unusual phrasings, etc.
2. Now listen to the recording while following along in the transcription. For those of you who have not had much experience with written music this may prove difficult, especially because Kenny plays many pieces at quite a healthy clip. Sadly enough, the only method of improving this skill is by practice.
3. At this point, pick up your fiddle and play through the first A and B parts. If you haven't had very much practice reading music you might want to concentrate solely on the rhythm and melody, leaving the bowing indications for a subsequent reading. If you come to a section that is hard to read, refer to the recording and see if that will clear up the problem. Once you have mastered the A and B parts, try some of the variations.

The Tunes

Big Sandy River
Kenny Baker Plays Bill Monroe

At one of Kenny's first recording sessions with the Bluegrass Boys, on December 6, 1962, Bill Monroe asked him if he had written a song that he would like to record. Kenny chose "Big Sandy River" (Decca 4382).* The transcription below is from a subsequent recording, *Kenny Baker Plays Bill Monroe*. This album was dedicated to Bill who has had, and continues to have, a major influence on Kenny's playing.

Kenny plays the B part basically in single bows. This, along with the fact that the melody is ascending and requires string-crossings at the beginning of each measure, can make for choppiness. To avoid this, use the upper half of the bow, and try crossing strings with the upper arm, from the shoulder, following as smooth a curve as possible while producing the up and down motion of the bow with the wrist.

Left to right: Kenny Baker, Joe Stewart, Bill Monroe.

*For a transcription of this version see: Stacy Phillips and Kenny Kosek, *Bluegrass Fiddle Styles* (New York: Oak Publications, 1978), p. 42.

Big Sandy River

Bill Monroe
Kenny Baker

© Copyright 1963 by Champion Music Corporation, New York, New York.
All Rights Reserved. Used by Permission

Notes:
B Parts 5 and 6, and 9 and 10 ≈ B and B2
A Parts 9 and 10 ≈ A and A2

Bluegrass in the Backwoods

Frost on the Pumpkin

The harmonic changes in this tune are more complex than those in most bluegrass tunes. The melody begins in D minor, then in the B part shifts into F major (D minor is the relative minor of F major). The C part reverts to D minor. The D part is surprising because it begins on the V chord (C) rather than on the I chord (F). This type of harmonic structure is common in both country ragtime and Western swing. For examples of this, listen to "Hawkin's Rag," "Dill Pickle Rag," or "Beaumont Rag."

Note the rubato introduction. To get a sense of its rhythm and dynamics listen closely to the recording. This may be easier than struggling with the ties in the written music. And as long as your copy of *Frost on the Pumpkin* is on the turntable, listen for Kenny's backup on the B part of the banjo break, achieved with long, luxurious bow strokes.

Copyright © 1978 by Southern Melody Publishing Co. All Rights Reserved. Used by Permission

Charmaine

Kenny Baker Country

Kenny first heard this piece performed by Stephane Grappelli, the legendary jazz violinist. The influence of jazz in Kenny's playing is particularly evident in his phrasing. In measure five, for example, the accent falls on the second half of the first beat of the measure instead of on the downbeat, where we expect it. This kind of shift in accent, or syncopated rhythm, is found throughout the piece (see measures eight, twenty-four, and thirty-three through forty-one), and contributes to its swing flavor.

At the Delaware Bluegrass Festival, 1972.

Charmaine

Copyright © Miller Music Corporation 1926; Renewed 1954.
International Copyright Secured. All Rights Reserved. Used by Permission.

Cross-Eyed Fiddler

A Baker's Dozen

This is another of Kenny's original compositions. At the beginning of the third measure, first attack the D with the fourth finger on the G string, then add in the open D right after it and play both Ds simultaneously. Let the fourth finger continue the drone for the duration of the measure.

The way in which double stops are played makes a big difference; both notes can be voiced equally, or one can be stressed more than the other. With this in mind, listen to measures fourteen and fifteen attentively, noting the difference in the emphasis on the double stops.

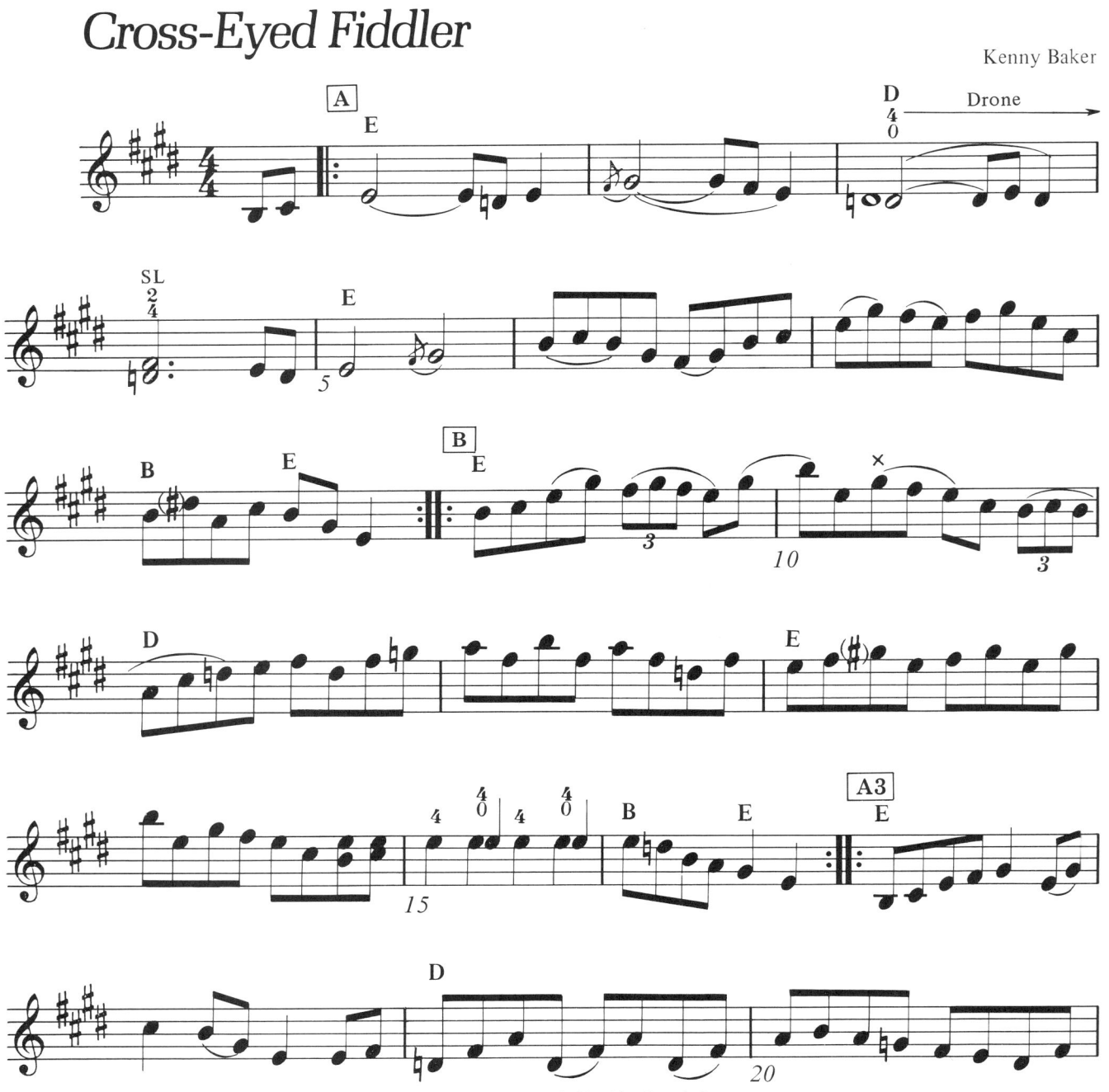

Copyright 1971 Wynwood Music Co., Inc. All Rights Reserved. Used by Permission.

A Parts 5 and 6, and 9 and 10 ≈ A and A2
B Parts 5 and 6, and 9 and 10 ≈ B and B2

Dead March

Bill Monroe's Uncle Pen

Bill Monroe had always wanted to record an album of the tunes he had learned from his Uncle Pen, but for a long time the key ingredient was lacking: a fiddler whom he thought could handle the material. When Kenny joined Monroe's band this problem was solved, and *Bill Monroe's Uncle Pen* has since become a classic bluegrass fiddle record. The "Dead March" is a double-fiddle piece; Kenny plays the melody, and Joe "Red" Hayes plays the harmony part.

Kenny's father (right) and brother, Carl, c. 1939.

Dead March

Bill Monroe

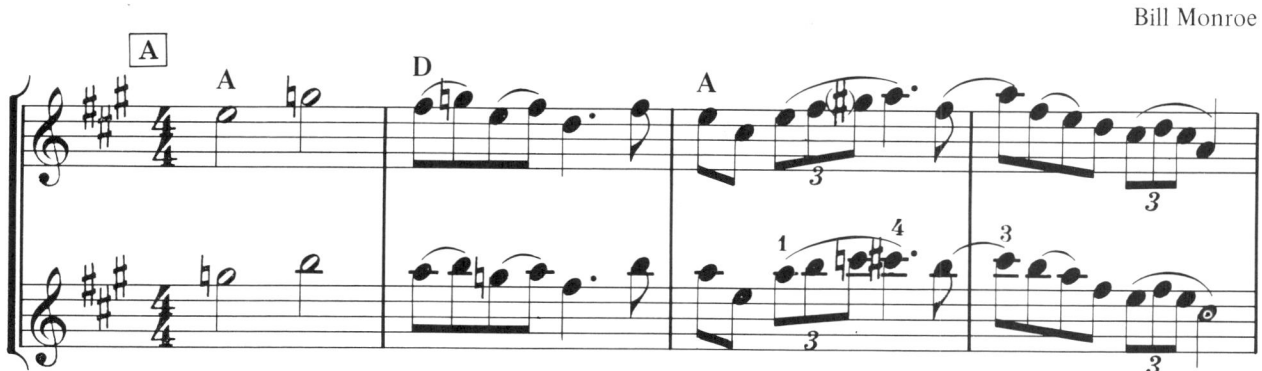
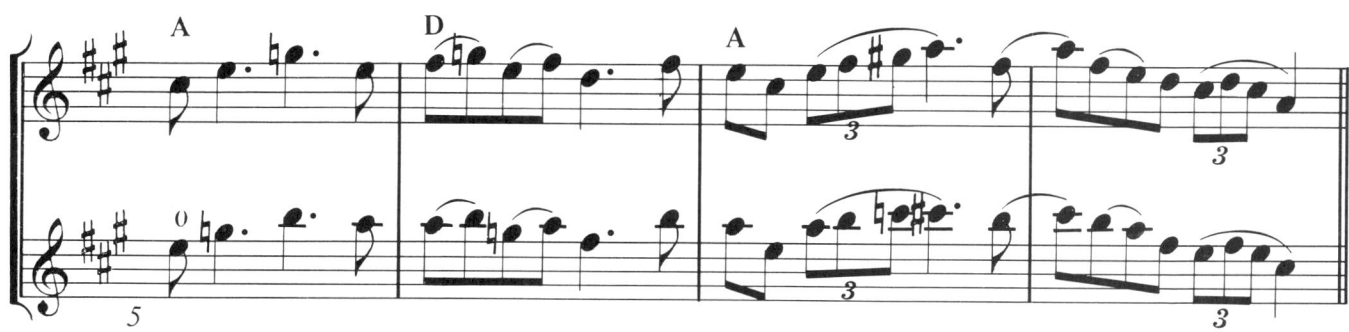
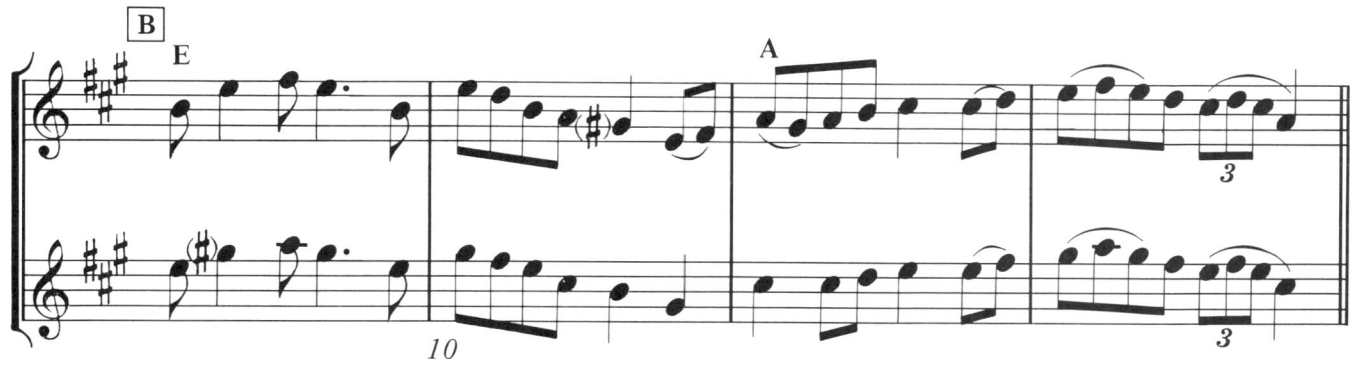
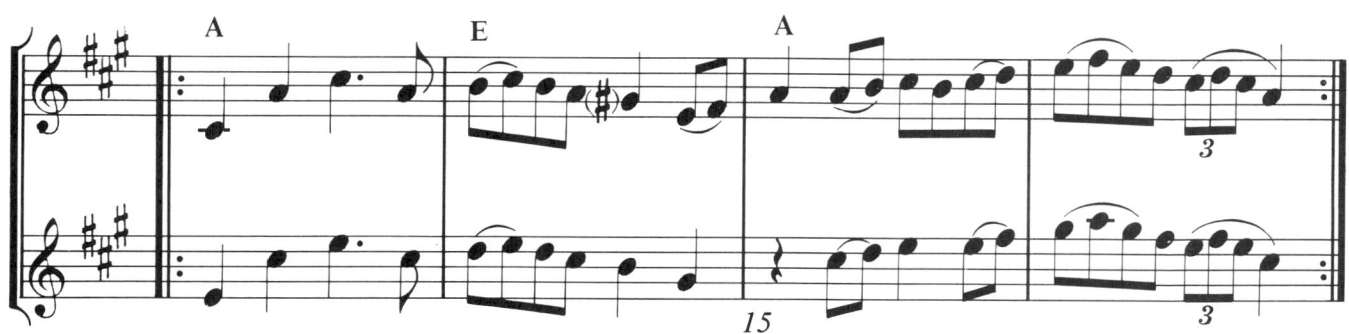

© Copyright 1973 by Bill Monroe Music. International Copyright Secured.
Made in U.S.A. All Rights Reserved. Used by Permission.

Denver Belle

A Baker's Dozen

Kenny Baker

Notes:
A4 and A10 ≈ A
A5 and A7 ≈ A3
A6 and A8 ≈ A2
A9 ≈ measures: 1 and 2 of A3, 3-6 of A2, and 7 and 8 of A
All B Parts are ≈ B

Doc Harris the Fisherman

A Baker's Dozen

Doc Harris, a Nashville fiddle maven, and old fishing buddy of Kenny's, is the source of the title of this most unusual tune. Here, as in "Bluegrass in the Backwoods," we have an interesting shift from minor to major. The B part begins with a B♭, the pivotal note in the modulation. One expects to move into the key of B♭ major, because G is its relative minor. Instead, the B♭ swings us into C, acting as a minor 7th, and giving the tune a blues flavor.

Both the third and seventh degrees of the scale are often played slightly flat to produce a "bluesy" sound. In this connection note the high B in measures nineteen and twenty-seven. Kenny cites Stephane Grappelli's "Minor Swing" as one of the main influences in the composition of this tune.

Doc Harris the Fisherman

Kenny Baker

Copyright 1971 Wynwood Music Co., Inc. All Rights Reserved. Used by Permission.

Done Gone
High Country

One of the astounding things about Kenny is his ability to re-fashion a tune and make it uniquely his own. His style cannot be ascribed to any region because his playing is not in essence imitative, but imaginative. The handling of phrases like the ones in measures twenty-three and twenty-four shows what is really distinctive about Kenny's playing of these old-time tunes. And that end tag! A prize piece of unmistakable Baker!

Kenny originally learned this tune from Marion Sumner, a fellow Kentucky fiddler who had a major influence on Kenny's early playing.

Done Gone

Arrangement © 1979 by Kenny Baker.

Notes:
A Parts 3 and 4 ≈ A and A2
A7 and A8 ≈ A5

Dry and Dusty

Dry and Dusty

Traditional

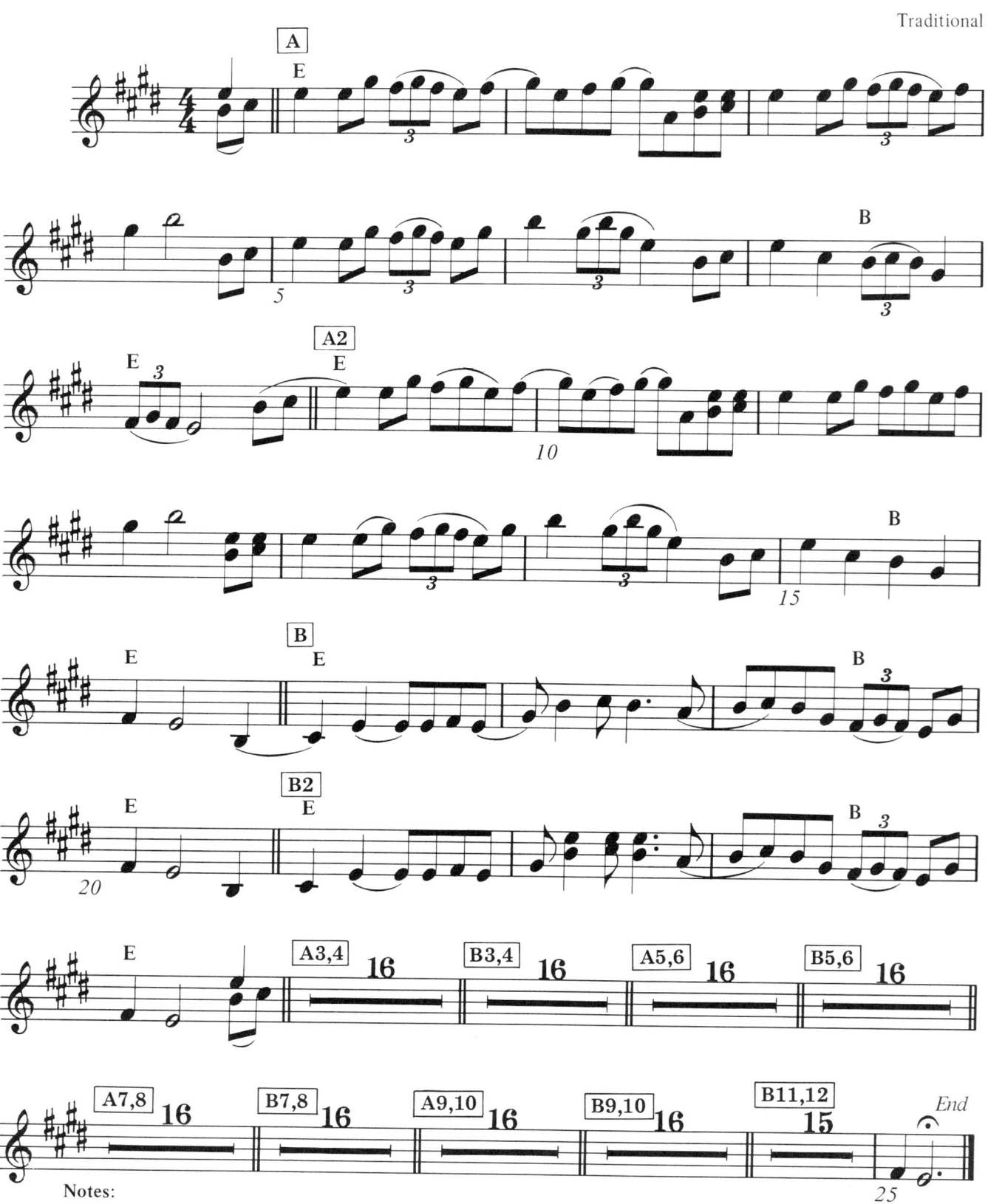

Notes:
All A and B Parts are played alike.

Arrangement © 1979 by Kenny Baker.

Ducks on the Millpond

Grassy Fiddle Blues

Kenny first heard this tune played by his father. He could remember only the A part, so he had to supply the other two parts himself.

The scale (or mode) on which this tune is built differs from that on which most Western music is based. A normal major scale, or Ionian mode, has half steps between the third and fourth, and seventh and eighth degrees of the scale, all other intervals being whole steps.

"Ducks on the Millpond" utilizes a scale with half steps occurring between the third and fourth, and sixth and seventh degrees of the scale. All other intervals are whole steps.

This mode, called Mixolydian, is commonly heard in Southern dance music.

Ducks on the Millpond

Kenny Baker

Copyright 1971 Wynwood Music Co., Inc. All Rights Reserved. Used by Permission.

Notes:
A Parts 5 and 6, and 7 and 8 ≈ A and A2
B Parts 3 and 4 ≈ B and B2
C Parts 3 and 4 ≈ C and C2

Festival Waltz

Kenny Baker Country

"The waltz is the place you can express yourself best," says Kenny. Part of this expressiveness is achieved through subtle dynamic changes which do not play an important role in the hoedowns.

The beauty of the waltz lies in the richness and smoothness of its execution, so be generous with the bow; use its full length. As Kenny's father T.E. used to say: "They don't put all that hair on it for nothing." Try measure twenty-one keeping this in mind. Starting at the frog, pull down to the very tip, simultaneously tracing a smooth arc with the upper arm. A little vibrato will help—indulge yourself, savor each note, and try to achieve a full and sonorous tone.

Kenny Baker, Bill Monroe, Tex Logan, Don Reno, Bill Harrel, et al.

Festival Waltz

Kenny Baker

Copyright 1972 Wynwood Music Co., Inc. All Rights Reserved. Used by Permission.

41

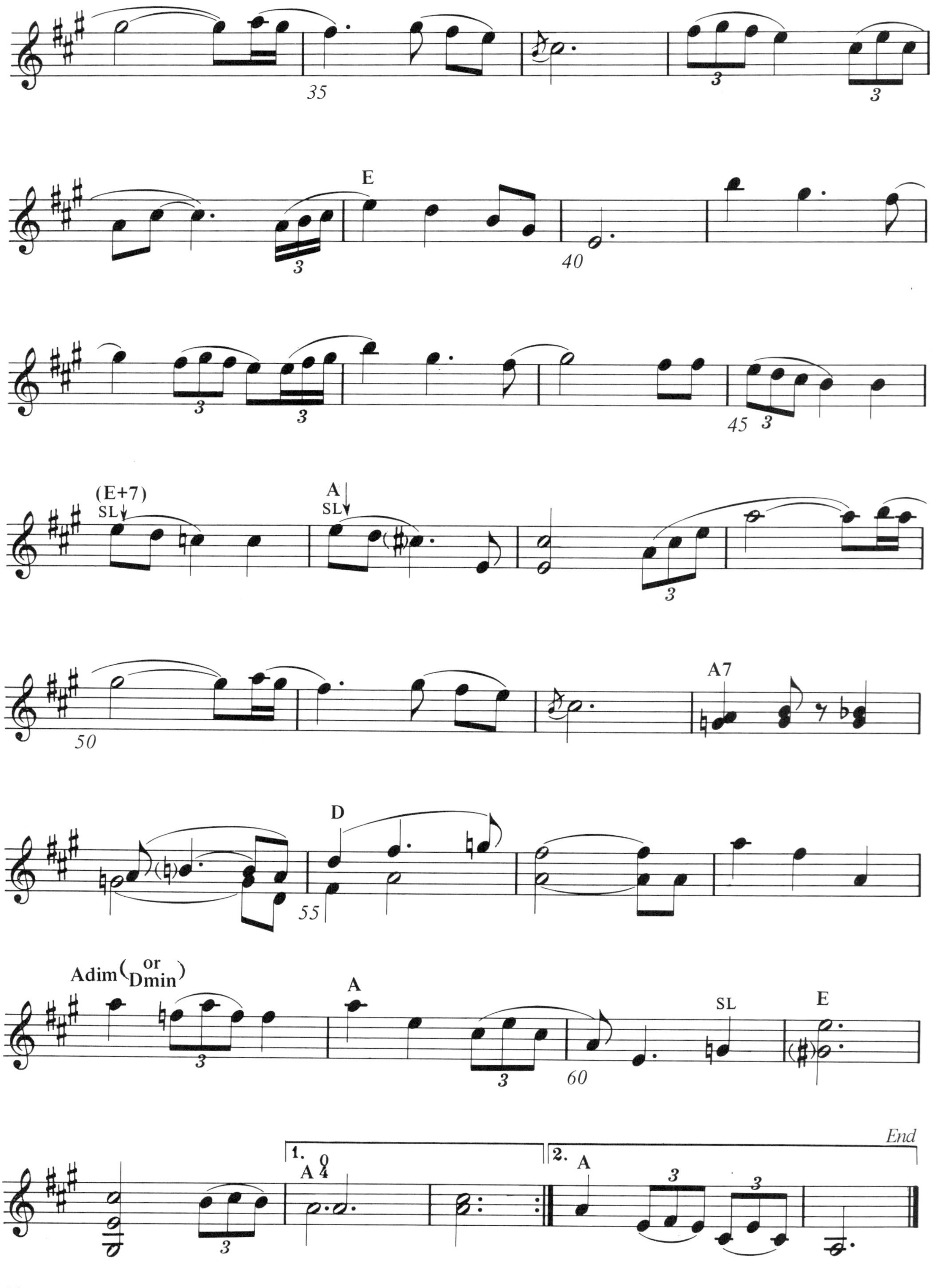
E
(E+7)
SL
A
SL
A7
D
Adim(or Dmin)
A
SL
E
1.
A 0 4
2.
A
End

First Day in Town

Portrait of a Bluegrass Fiddler

On March 14, 1968, Kenny went back to playing with Bill Monroe. He checked into a motel in Nashville and, having some time to kill before their engagement, wrote this tune.

In C5 and 6 and in B5 and 6 a variation is added using a shuffle on a G minor double stop: B♭, first finger on the A string; and G, third finger on the D string.

First Day in Town

Kenny Baker

Copyright 1969 Wynwood Music Co., Inc. All Rights Reserved. Used by Permission.

Notes:
A Parts 3 and 4 ≈ A and A2
B Parts 3 and 4, 5 and 6, and 7 and 8 ≈ B and B2
C Parts 3 and 4, 5 and 6, and 7 and 8 ≈ C and C2

Flopareno

Grassy Fiddle Blues

After taping the material that he planned to use on *Grassy Fiddle Blues,* Kenny realized that he needed one more tune to make the record complete. He came up with "Flopareno" on the spot. Like "Charmaine" it has a jazzy sort of phrasing. See for example the irregular accent patterns in measures nineteen, and ninety-seven and ninety-eight. And like "Charmaine," it too has a single melody line (unlike the fiddle tunes which are in binary form), which is the basis for some stunning improvisation.

Joe Stuart named the tune in honor of Kenny whom he used to call by the nickname "Flopareno."

Flopareno

Kenny Baker

Copyright 1975 Wynwood Music Co., Inc. All Rights Reserved. Used by Permission.

II
D
Bdim(or G7)
SL
D
E
A
SL
SL
A7
D
Bdim(or G7)
D
III
D
Bdim(or G7)
D
E
A
D
Bdim(or G7)
D

IV
D
Bdim(or G7)
D
50
E
3
55
A
SL
SL
A7
D
Bdim(or G7)
D
60
V
D
Bdim(or G7)
SL
D
65
E
SL
1 3
2 4
70
A
SL
SL
75
A7
D
Bdim(or G7)
D

VI
D
Bdim (or G7)
SL
D
80
E
3
85
A
SL
SL
90
A7
D
Bdim (or G7)
D
95
VII
D
Bdim (or G7)
D
100
E
SL
SL
3
A
105
3
3
3
A7
D
Bdim (or G7)
110
D

49

Grey Eagle
Dry and Dusty

This is a popular traditional tune among bluegrass, old-timey, and Texas fiddlers. Kenny first heard this one done by Howdy Forrester, a fiddler whom he has always admired.

This version involves a set of variations on the basic melody which requires shifting from first to third position, and from third to fourth position (with the fourth finger). If you haven't had much experience in shifting positions, try these variations using a basic saw stroke (one note for each bow), and playing the melody slowly at first. Doing it this way provides an excellent exercise in intonation.

Grey Eagle

Traditional

Arrangement © 1979 by Kenny Baker

D
A
E
20
A
D
A
E
A
A3,4
Banjo
16
B3,4
16
C1,2
16
A5,6
Fiddle
16
B5,6
16
C3,4
A
25
E
A
30
SL
1.
E
A
2.
E
A
D
A
35
E
SL
E
A
E
A
40

Notes:
A Parts 5 and 6 ≈ ‖: A :‖
B Parts 5 and 6 ≈ B and B2

Indian Killed a Woodcock
A Baker's Dozen

Kenny learned this tune from his father, who had a major influence on his playing. T.E. played with a "long bow style" instead of the shuffle style which was prevalent in his time.

Indian Killed a Woodcock

Kenny Baker

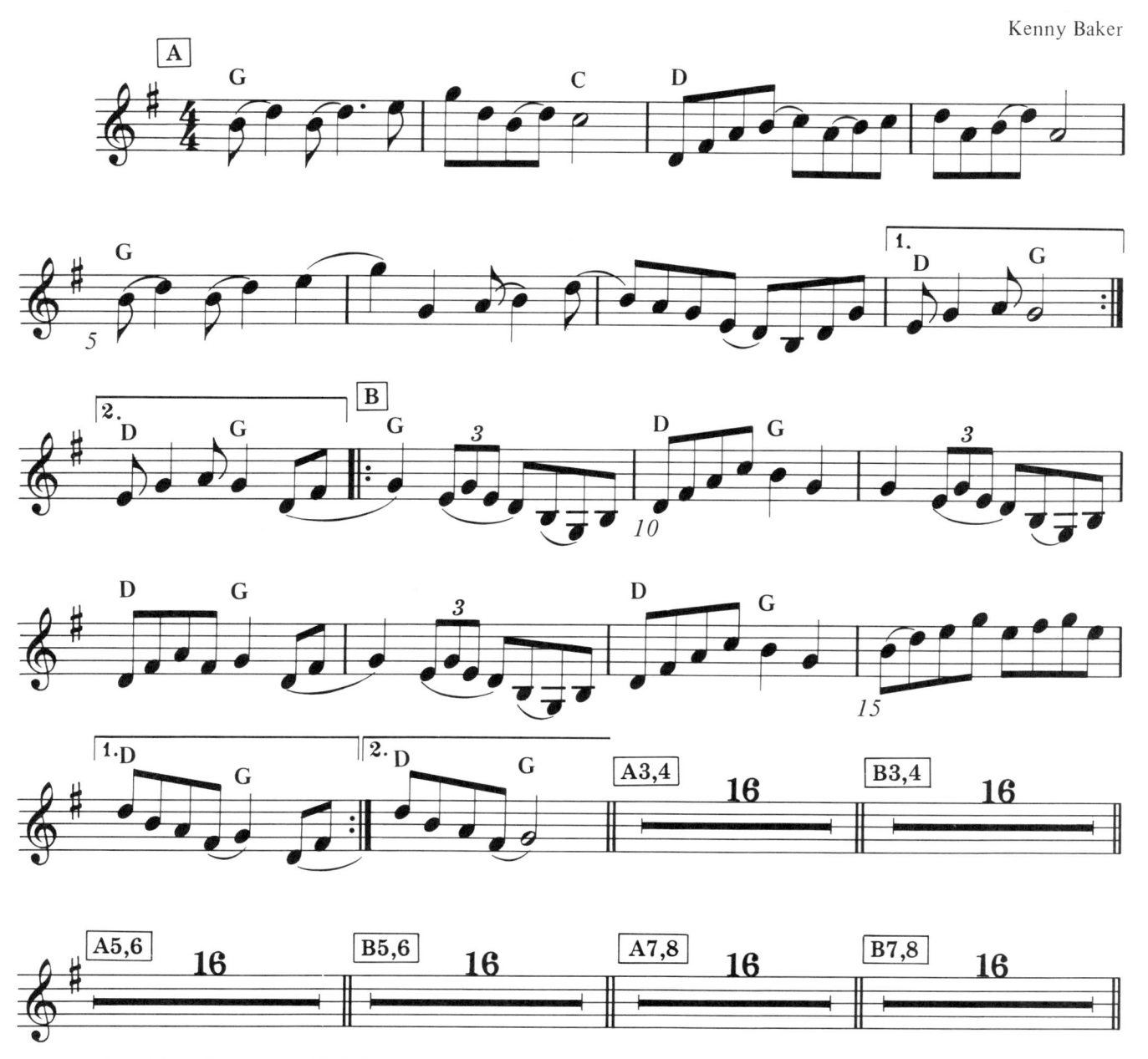

Copyright 1971 Wynwood Music Co., Inc. All Rights Reserved. Used by Permission.

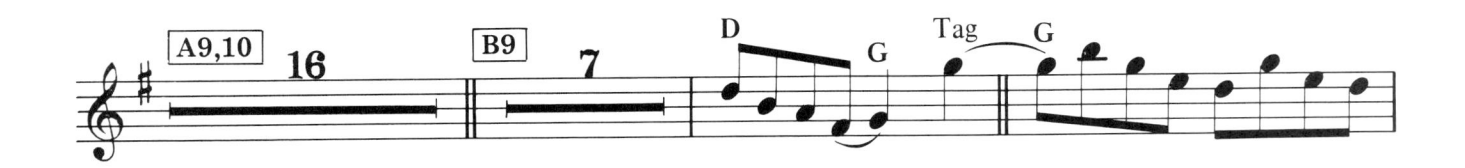

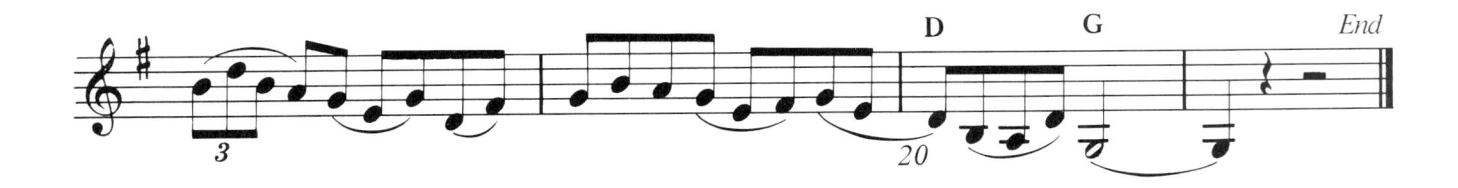

Notes:
Except for the variations indicated below, Kenny plays all A and B Parts alike.

Some Variations:
the first measure of A2

the first measure of A6

the first measures of B5 and 6

Johnny the Blacksmith

A Baker's Dozen

One of the things Kenny enjoys about working with Monroe is that Bill may play the same song any number of times, yet handle it in a variety of ways. By so doing he keeps the tune fresh, so that it remains a challenge. Kenny has a similar sense in regard to his own music. He has in mind a strong but rough outline of what he wants to do and hear in a piece, but the exact choice of melody, tempo, rhythm, and phrasing comes to him as he plays it. This recording of "Johnny the Blacksmith" is a good example of this attitude. Although Kenny had played it many times before, this is the first time he did it as a fast hoedown.

Johnny the Blacksmith

Kenny Baker

Copyright 1971 Wynwood Music Co., Inc. All Rights Reserved. Used by Permission.

Notes:
A Parts 3 and 4, 5 and 6, 7 and 8, 9 and 10, and 11 and 12 ≈ A and A2
B Parts 3 and 4, 5 and 6, 7 and 8, 9 and 10, and 11 and 12 ≈ B and B2

Lee Wedding Tune

Bill Monroe's Uncle Pen

Bill Monroe

© Copyright 1973 by Bill Monroe Music. International Copyright Secured.
Made in U.S.A. All Rights Reserved. Used by Permission.

Notes:
B6 ≈ B
A Parts 9 and 10 ≈ A and A2
B Parts 9 and 10 ≈ B and B2

Missouri Road

Grassy Fiddle Blues

Here is another tune with a touch of swing to it. As mentioned above (c.f. "Doc Harris the Fisherman") the third degree of the scale is often played a touch flat to contribute a bluesy sound. We find this "blues third" in measures thirty and forty-six where the D is played a trifle flat.

Missouri Road

Kenny Baker

Copyright 1976 Wynwood Music Co., Inc. All Rights Reserved. Used by Permission.

Notes:
A Parts 2 and 4 ≈ A, but measures 1, 5, and 9 are played without double stops.
A3 ≈ A
B3 ≈ B
B4 ≈ B, but measures 23-4 are played like this.

Mule Skinner Blues

Bill Monroe's Country Music Hall of Fame

This recording is hard to find but well worth the search. Kenny's breaks on "Mule Skinner Blues" and "Rocky Road Blues"* (another tune on the album) are outstanding by any standard: every aspiring bluegrass fiddler will want to hear them. Here again, the phrasing is of great interest. In both the third and fourth measures the accent falls on the second beat, (in the fourth measure the accent falls on the latter half of the second beat). In measures thirty-five and thirty-six Kenny introduces a syncopated rhythm of three-into-four, so that the accent is in constant motion. Counting each eighth note it falls first on the 1st, then on the 4th, then on the 7th then on the 2nd, and then on the 5th eighth note.

The parts marked I, III, and V are breaks; II, IV, and VI are backup. Be careful when beginning the tune. You will need the whole bow, so start at the frog.

Mule Skinner Blues

Jimmie Rodgers
George Vaughn

Copyright 1931 by Peer International Corporation. Copyright Renewed.
Copyright 1950 by Peer International Corporation. Copyright Renewed. Used by Permission.

*Phillips and Kosek, *Bluegrass Fiddle Styles*, p. 71.

62

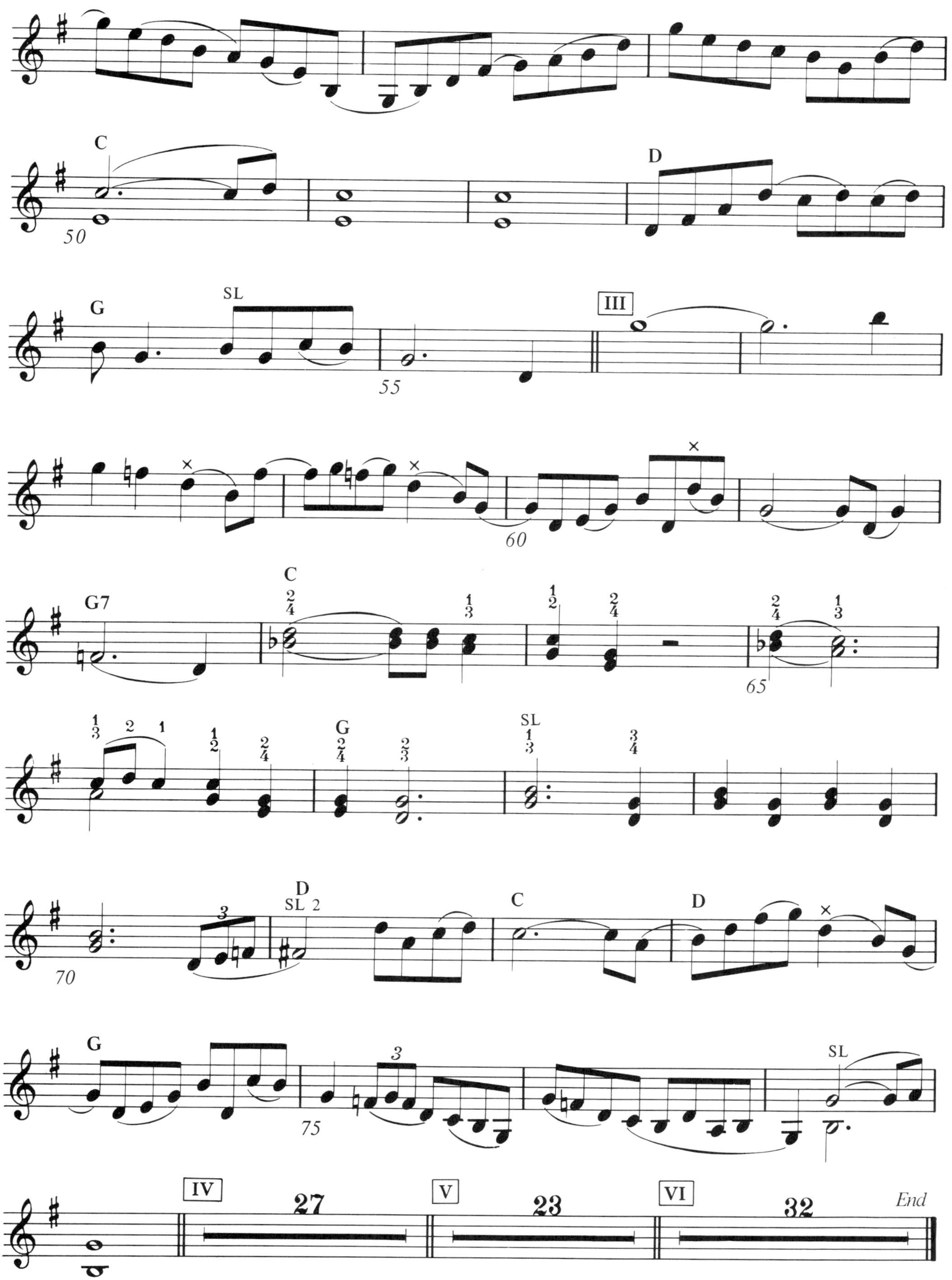
C
50
D
G
SL
55
III
60
G7
C
65
G
SL
70
D
SL 2
C
D
G
75
SL
IV
27
V
23
VI
32
End

Notes:
Part IV ≈ II, but substitute below for measures 35-43

and this for 52-55

Part V ≈ I, but substitute this for measures 9 and 10

Part VI ≈ II, but substitute below for measures 37-43

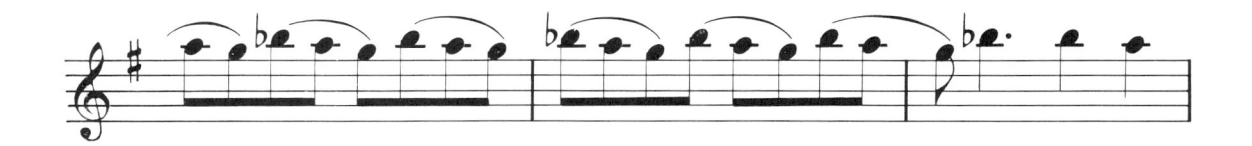

Sail Away Ladies

A Baker's Dozen

Kenny's father played a version similar to this, and although T.E. rarely played with a guitar accompaniment, Kenny always heard these chords behind it.

Sail Away Ladies

Traditional

Arrangement © 1979 by Kenny Baker

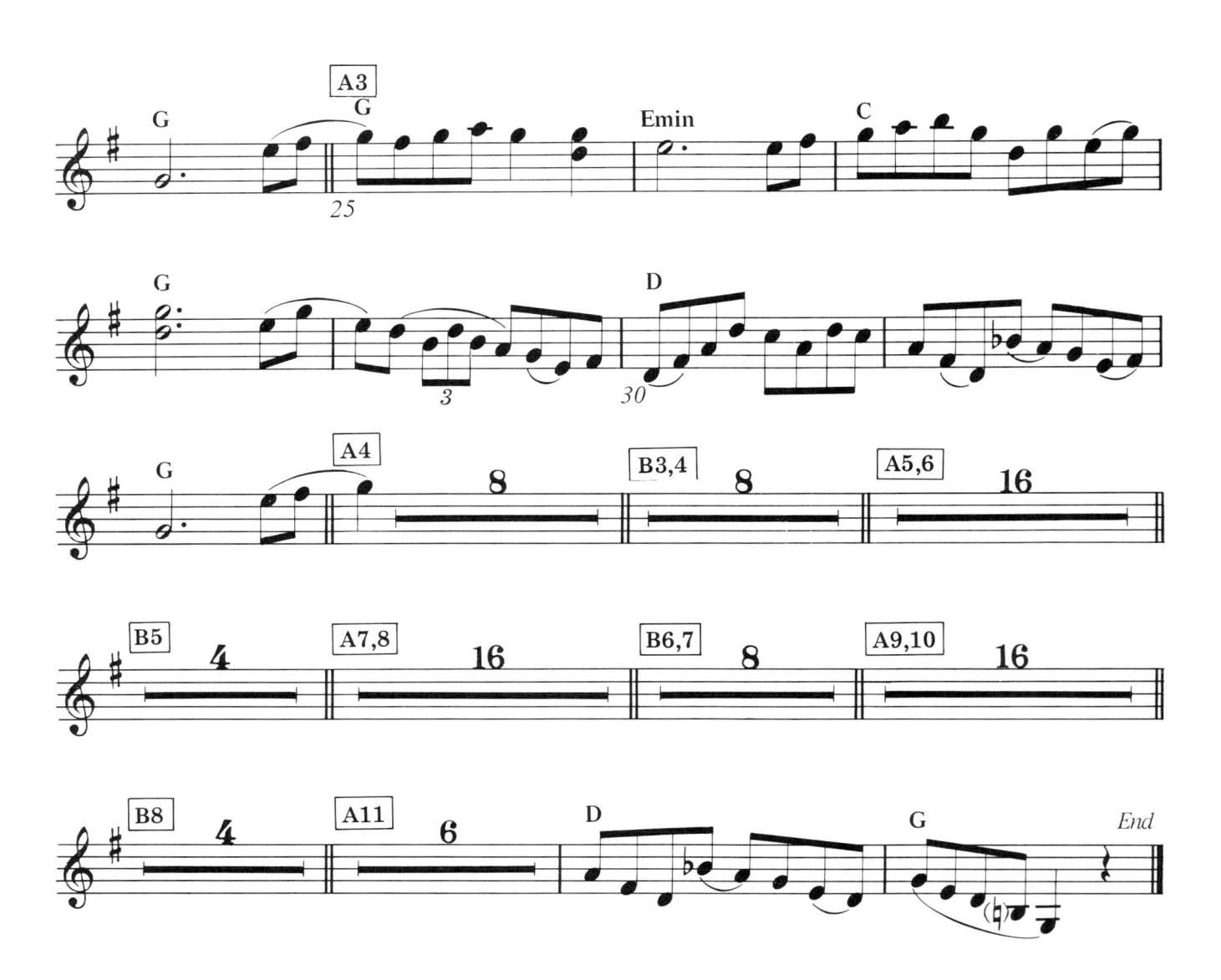

Notes:
A4 and A11 ≈ A3
All Bs ≈ B
A Parts 5 and 6, 7 and 8, and 9 and 10 ≈ A and A2

Salty

Kenny Baker Country

Besides being a great tune, this Baker original is chock-full of nifty licks that are well worth knowing, especially those in measures twenty-one and twenty-two, and in twenty-five and twenty-six. The phrase in measures forty-five and forty-six is a real gem and can be used in any G E A D progression. Try it in "Georgia Brown"—it will really swing.

Pay special attention to the way each phrase begins and ends. In measures one, five, nine, thirteen, seventeen, and twenty-one there is an assertiveness in the attack which separates them from the preceding phrases. Likewise, at the end of certain phrases there is a dynamic tapering off, or a hint of a rest; listen to measures four, eight, twelve, sixteen, and twenty. This use of dynamics as a phrasing device can change a group of running eighth notes into an exciting melody.

Salty

Kenny Baker

Notes:
A3 ≈ A2
A4 ≈ A2, but with this new first measure

The first eight measures of B3 ≈ B12-24, the second eight measures are ≈ B2 49-56
C2 ≈ C

Spider Bit the Baby

Kenny Baker Country

Kenny was home on his farm one day working on this tune when he noticed a rather large spider crawling down the wall. If nothing else, it gave him an idea for a title that was meant to parody "Rattlesnake Bit the Baby."

Spider Bit the Baby

Kenny Baker

Copyright 1972 Wynwood Music Co., Inc. All Rights Reserved. Used by Permission.

Notes:
A Parts 11 and 12 ≈ A and A2
A Parts 5 and 6, 7 and 8, and 9 and 10 ≈ A3 and A4
B Parts 3 and 4, 5 and 6, and 7 and 8 ≈ B and B2

Kenny plays A and A2 in second position. If you haven't had much experience playing in this position it may prove difficult at first, but once mastered it makes the piece easier to play. You begin like this:

Discography

This discography is limited to those records that were used in the preparation of this book.

Solo Albums:

Portrait of a Bluegrass Fiddler	County 719
A Baker's Dozen	County 730
Kenny Baker Country	County 736
Dry and Dusty	County 744
Grassy Fiddle Blues	County 750
Kenny Baker Plays Bill Monroe	County 761
Frost on the Pumpkin	County 770

With Other Artists:

Bill Monroe's Uncle Pen	Decca D17-5348
Bill Monroe's Country Music Hall of Fame	Decca D1-75281
High Country (Kenny Baker and Joe Greene)	County 714

The albums on the County label can be ordered from two sources:

County Records   Roundup Records
Box 191   or   Box 474
Floyd, VA 24091   Somerville, MA 02144

You are most likely to find the albums on the Decca label in the bluegrass section of any large record store.

For more transcriptions of Kenny Baker's playing, see:

Matt Glaser *Teach Yourself Bluegrass Fiddle* (New York: Amsco Music Publishing Company, 1978), p. 51.

Stacy Phillips and Kenny Kosek, *Bluegrass Fiddle Styles* (New York: Oak Publications, 1978), pp. 42, 44, 70, 71, 72, 94, 100, 103.